DOES A YAK GET A HAIRCUT?

Fred Ehrlich, M.D.
Pictures by Emily Bolam

🍎 **Blue Apple Books**

Maplewood, N.J.

For Will & Nate

Text copyright © 2003 by Fred Ehrlich, M.D.
Illustrations copyright © 2003 by Emily Bolam
All rights reserved
CIP Data is available.

Published in the United States 2003 by
🍎 Blue Apple Books
515 Valley Street, Maplewood, N.J. 07040
www.blueapplebooks.com
An affiliate of Handprint Books
Distributed in the U.S. by Chronicle Books

First Edition
Printed in China
ISBN: 1-59354-016-7

1 3 5 7 9 10 8 6 4 2

Who gets a haircut?
Does a yak?

Oh, no!

A yak is supposed to have long hair.
It keeps him warm where it's
snowy and very cold.

Does a rhinoceros get a haircut?

No indeed!
A rhinoceros has thick skin
and not much hair.

Does a whale get a haircut?

No way! A whale has no hair at all.

Instead it has a thick layer of fat,
called blubber, to keep it warm.

Which animals do get haircuts?

Sheep are sheared for their wool.

Goats are clipped to keep them cool in summer.

So are dogs.

Some owners take their dogs
for special haircuts.

"You're such a neat poodle," says Polly.
"Are you ready for your treat?"

People get their hair cut too.
Some get their hair trimmed at home.

Others get their hair cut and styled
at a barbershop or beauty salon.

Some kids like to get their hair cut;

some kids don't like it at all!

Will likes to get his hair cut.
When he's finished clipping and cutting,
the barber says, "See you in six weeks."

"How do you know?" asks Will.

The barber says, "Hair grows a little every day. In a month your hair will be at least one-half inch longer."

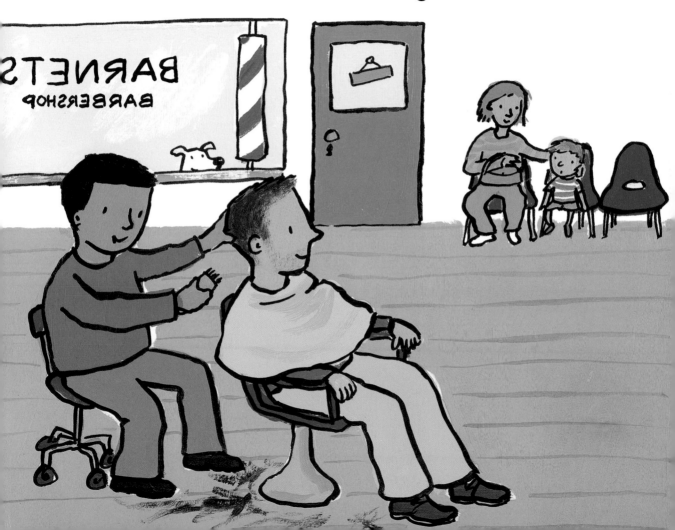

"Is hair dead or alive?" asks Will.

"Both! It's alive at the roots and dead at the ends where I cut."

"So that's why it hurts when my brother pulls my hair!"

"And that's why a haircut
never hurts anybody!"